MERIDIAN

Tupelo Press Snowbound Series
Chapbook Award Winners

Barbara Tran, *In the Mynah Bird's Own Words*
Selected by Robert Wrigley

David Hernandez, *A House Waiting for Music*
Selected by Ray Gonzalez

Mark Yakich, *The Making of Collateral Beauty*
Selected by Mary Ruefle

Joy Katz, *The Garden Room*
Selected by Lisa Russ Spaar

Cecilia Woloch, *Narcissus*
Selected by Marie Howe

John Cross, *staring at the animal*
Selected by Gillian Conoley

Stacey Waite, *the lake has no saint*
Selected by Dana Levin

Brandon Som, *Babel's Moon*
Selected by Aimee Nezhukumatathil

Kathleen Jesme, *Meridian*
Selected by Patricia Fargnoli

MERIDIAN

Kathleen Jesme

TUPELO PRESS

North Adams, Massachusetts

TUPELO PRESS
P.O. Box 1767, North Adams, Massachusetts 01247
Telephone: (413) 664-9611 / Fax: (413) 664-9711
editor@tupelopress.org / www.tupelopress.org

Tupelo Press is an award-winning independent literary press that publishes fine fiction, non-fiction, and poetry in books that are a joy to hold as well as read. Tupelo Press is a registered 501(c)3 non-profit organization, and we rely on public support to carry out our mission of publishing extraordinary work that may be outside the realm of the large commercial publishers. Financial donations are welcome and are tax deductible.

MERIDIAN

1

Late, very late. The year displaces
itself. Bits and pieces. Winter evenings, a sense
of waiting
   overtakes her.

She is close to the owls: they love
                        winter for its wakefulness
and plentiful food, the long hunting
hours, clear tracks of mice

over the moon-white snow.
               She opens her mouth.   Song a lamp
shining into the oblique
dark, comes.

~

I left the cemetery
knee-deep

the snow laying a wreath
and then blotting it.

~

It snowed for four days in the middle of January, during which my mother lay dying. Every time I left her little apartment, my car had changed shapes again. It was too cold to snow, but it snowed. So the snow was light: I could almost blow the car clean of it with my breath. I wore the boots of that city—mukluks, which are good in the constant snow. Some people go barefoot inside their mukluks. I wonder if they are thinking of sand and summer. There was no risk of thaw.

~

It was snowing

and it snowed:

one snow fell

down inside

the other, two flocks

of gulls alighting

on a white beach. Each

fell and replaced

the other.

~

Anyone deaf, who couldn't
  see what was going on
               was her mother
who had outlived
             her life and still
kept living. Anyone
      deaf, anyone blind
  who couldn't even then
                 who didn't even then.

~

Two days with black edges. Straight lines
a mourning.   They say *evergreen*
but what I see is black, now
that I am looking, just
      remnants fallen
under the double spell of obliteration and imprint.

~

The days had darkened.
Everything the same.
Except her. She was older, sadder, sooner. Still she
passed the time
with singing.

~

There was no risk of winter ending, or even letting up momentarily. Before, she had eaten and drunk liquids. She had spoken to people. She had even played her piano every day, although some days her left hand rested on her right and she seemed not to notice it. On those days, it was only melody that she picked out. On the days when she had two hands, she played just as she used to, old tunes for sing-along, with an airy touch, never landing hard on any key. Now, there was no possibility of any more piano playing. She no longer sat up or tried to get out of bed, no longer opened her eyes. She was breathing through her mouth, lightly but quickly.

~

I walked into that room
          and found the furniture
                    had been removed and all
                              the windows broken out.
          Someone with stones. The wind blew
                    through as if it had a right
and made square sounds.
                    The wind had been tamed
          by the things we construct
    to box in and out, the shapes
of buildings, window frames.

~

She was becoming a dead person, but she hadn't yet arrived. And there were few similarities, other than the familiar smell of her body, to what she had once been. My father, as I recall, smelled like saltwater in summer and in winter like old wool and wild game.

~

2:22. There isn't much here but a spoon
and a hand with an arm to lift it.
A mouth. Soup. Salt.

Reverse evaporation
would net potable water
with no salt in it. There
are some things we
can't. Reverse. But.

~

She was wandering along

an imaginary line
trying to find
her way. She was poles
apart from herself.
Nobody would give her
the latitude to make
a mistake. But that's
what she needed.

2

It's as if the snow
looked in and whispered
among itselves
oh look there
at the lights,

something snow
knows little about
except as a
receiver of day,
which it dutifully
holds all night
even on the
darkest nights,
which these are.

~

I kept leaving and leaving her apartment, two tiny rooms with a large
grand piano taking up most of one, a hospital bed and dresser filling
the other. It felt as if I were always leaving. Yet I was coming. For
every time I left, I had already come. *Come* is always followed by
leave, although the reverse is not necessarily true.

~

Traveling north again, into winter, she walks
through small towns on the edge
of extinction, wind scrubbing
paint from buildings
that lean forward
to listen.

In the black distance a single light,
rectangle of an open door.

~

You have come
to the end of that thought
and require a new one

you live by one thought
alone until
it dries up and blows
off, a pod in wind

~

In addition to the piano, there were two chairs and a television in the farther room. My mother could not watch; she was peripherally sighted, but anything she tried to look at disappeared in the blank at the center. In the last months, she was unable to track anything more complicated than a single sentence.

~

White dog in winter:
his bark is all that's
visible

~

A year after the ankle injury,
she retraces her footprints
on the path by the white spruce
trees. Her left
foot angles out;
the right goes pretty much
forward.

                                        But she is taken
                                        aside, ever so
                            slightly, by each left step.

Somewhere along the line of trees
something
changes
into language.

~

In the city where my mother died, no one plows the streets. Instead,
vehicles drive over the snow until it is flattened into ice and becomes
part of the roadway. In spring, the last things to melt are the
streets. Late April, with bare lawns and boulevards, patches of snow
retreating in shade, and the roads still white and rutted, as the path
remains where I walk all winter and where the dogs run, tamping
down the snow solid to be the last trace of winter.

~

I think I hear her say, "I mean nothing
by this

mean hovel
mean scrape
and trowel

mean gather beads
and string
them—"

~

I mean nothing:

the real first word
is *M*

and it means
"to be separated."

~

Once, when I came out from the small apartment where my mother lay dying, everything had become so white I couldn't make out the buildings, the streets, or the place where the sky and ground met. I got in my car hoping to orient myself with its sturdy accoutrements, but it was not until I was driving, feeling the wheels under me on the road, that up and down became clear.

3

She remembers, from far away, the anhingas,
the storks, roseate spoonbill
stalking the shallows,
perfectly suited to
what they do.

She watches the local birds, the ones
that are left—and those
that come from farther
north to winter here
in snow and
darkness;

                    at night listens to the slow hoot of the great-horned owl
                                    beginning its January courtship.

She considers the lack of twilight.
The sun falls fat below the girth
of earth. Everything strays,
   indirect slant
         partial circuitous
               tortuous oblique.
                     A circus of hints.
                           Easily obliterated.

~

Eight seconds more of daylight
than yesterday
make all the
difference: song begins.

Moon almost full
setting at 8 a.m.
into the white spruce
drained of color.

~

But today sun layers   blue shadows
on white ground   pawprints
in the new snow   bird shadows
in shadow trees

that world   the one full
of shadows   the one that exists only
in winter

~

Sometime during the first or second night after my sister and I arrived in the city where my mother died, she called out at night, "Help me!" My sister was there, napping in my father's old recliner. What could she do? Moisten her open mouth, stroke her hair, hold her hand. Those were the only words my mother said during the time of her dying.

~

She is not interested in bringing home
shells or the island made
from shells
shells piled on the beach
making more sand.
They are all dead. She cares
instead about the silvery
fish leaping in the bays
and shallows

long shiny fish leaping
because fish
want to fly.

~

I played her piano, badly, old tunes by ear—and my mother, in the other room, without opening her eyes, lifted her arms and began to conduct the music, her habit as the church choir director. My sister watched her while I played so she could remember. But it was easier to sing. I could sit beside her and watch her face, hold her hand. I sang every old song I knew, then went to her piano bench and found a few more. I sang them all, over and over:

My bonny lies over the ocean
Someone's in the kitchen with Dinah
Danny boy
Doodle-de-doo
Down by the old millstream
Tell me why
Pop goes the weasel

Once, she lifted her hands and clapped them together slowly three times.

~

At the edge
of imagination

no, the edge
of memory
which goes back farther
than imagination—

and yet she thinks of it
throws the dog a ball
washes the dinner dishes
opens up a book

and continues in all
the usual ways.

~

Wilde's last words were "Either that wallpaper goes or I do!" Brahms said, "Ah, that tastes nice. Thank you." And Dickinson: "I must go in, the fog is rising." Many years ago, my father died alone, outdoors, which he would have liked, and he may, earlier in the morning, have said something like "Below zero this morning," or "See you later," to the neighbor with whom he'd eaten breakfast at the café.

4

At the piano Pletnev
grounds
the music
with himself

A quiet second
movement
one note, then
a leaping sixth

awkward melody
with left hand far below—

everything difficult
for Beethoven—

〜

The day my mother died, she was nearly entirely purple, including
most of her face, and her tiny body looked slender as a child's. Her
facial wrinkles smoothed away. She was developing bedsores from
being on her left side too long. It was the only position in which she
could breathe easily. I was losing my courage.

~

Destiny? Providence.
Fortune. Luck. Some

are names for gods.

~

A softness at the core
that makes one
vulnerable to the
hardness of the world.

~

Tuning a piano is a simple frequency calibration done with the
human ear. The tuner compares a standard musical pitch to the
same note on the keyboard. The smallest frequency offset a piano
tuner can hear depends on many factors: volume, duration of tone,
suddenness of frequency change, the musical training of the listener.

~

I thought her heart could not keep on so long. In the afternoon, knowing that she would have to die that day, I left and returned to my brother's house. I spent the rest of the day writing her obituary. She had prepared all of the material she wanted included, her significant dates—with only date of death left blank—the events of her life that mattered to her. She had collected samples of other obituaries whose style or format she liked, and I had only to select one as a model and piece together her life. For her funeral, she had listed everything she wanted—but had done this over and over, each time forgetting that she had already made these plans, so that I had to pick which to use, and I picked one with all of the people still alive, and capable of carrying a coffin, or singing, or attending.

~

Then, at the end of the day,
a quiet little coda:
A = 440 cycles per second
and 880 cycles, among others.
A at the beginning
and in the middle,
and also at the end.

~

A great circle
  of the celestial sphere

that passes through the celestial poles
  and the zenith of the

observer.

~

Fetal horses
gallop in the womb

I am swimming toward you
through

the past
which clings to me
and holds me
back
and up.

~

After dinner at my brother's house, I didn't go back to the tiny apartment, although I knew that she would have to die that night. I went to bed in my nephew's room, a large corner bedroom, nearly empty, my mother's dressing table with its large mirror looking very out of place. I went to sleep, a dreamless dark from which I was wakened at 11:30. I hurried to dress, but felt as if I were moving through deep snow. I put on my coat and boots, and drove through the falling snow to where my mother's body and my sister and brother waited for me. I smoothed her hair back and kissed her forehead, which was still warm. She still smelled like my mother. Someone from hospice would be coming from a nearby town in about an hour. We called the funeral home in our home town to send someone to pick up the body. The body—already not my mother. She didn't speak French any more. She didn't play the piano any more. She was already not. It felt sudden.

~

coeli, coeli

sky/ heaven/ heavens; space air/ climate/ weather; universe/world

out of the blue

pleni sunt coeli

et terra et terra—don't forget terra—

gloria ejus

are filled with your glory

heaven and earth

pleni sunt coeli et terra

words that suddenly ripen
and drop to the ground

pleni sunt coeli et terra

5

Listen: the even thump
of the bread maker mixing
  dough.
Hot rolls with supper. Home,
its dreary domestic
  pleasures.

~

We had decided my mother would not be on view. I had been asking
my sister to pick something out for two days, afraid that, after the
death, she would not be able to complete the task. But she refused to
look until afterwards. I would have chosen a sweat suit, something
practical and comfortable. My sister fretted through the closet,
pulling out and rejecting suit jackets with no matching skirts, dresses
with food stains or rips. Finally, she selected a two-toned lavender
silk dress, elegant, suitable for a wedding, a dress in which my
mother had been photographed, although I cannot remember the
occasion.

~

The wading birds, their long long legs, rapier beaks,
the digging wood storks
that scratch up the bottom
and stick their beaks in,
the gregarious ibises
hanging around,
opportunistic.

~

In the field behind my house, they are digging a deep pit to lay a
sewer line. Every few minutes, a loud shuddering-grinding sound
replaces the semi-rural quiet. More than forty trees of my small
woods have yielded to the incursion of pipes seventy feet below. "You
can plant more trees when we're done," the construction foreman
explains. I do not answer that trees are not identical, not replaceable.
I must walk back there and look past the orange snow fence and
down into the hole. I tell myself that every day.

~

Musics invariably clash but so do
silences.

The middle sphere echoes with their disparate,
far-flung ringing.

Pressed forward by sound and held back
by the gaps between the notes

variation and theme coerce time.

~

The empty
vessel rings: *nothing* sounds
while *something*
doesn't.

~

Everything must still

~

Only the extraneous details remain. Before my mother started to die, I didn't notice the dark purpling under her fingernails, although I did notice that no one seemed to be combing her hair any more. She herself had forgotten about hair. I did notice that sometimes she appeared not to know who I was, while at other times, she hugged me and said, "You love me; I know you do." Those are the minutiae.

~

Made by the eyes, looking, the observer, seeing:

a line that passes through
all of us, our poles.

~

It was a stone's throw

a distance dependent

on the arm of the

one heaving the stone

and how it went through

the yielding window

breaking it out

~

I did not want to look at her dead again. At the time, there was no option to retrieve the image of her living. Since then, I have noticed the dead image gradually recede in its brutal clarity, although not entirely, to be replaced more often with a picture or scene from before, when my mother might have smiled, spoken, frowned, or in some other way demonstrated life.

~

Holding back
with each silence
each rest induces
time to slow
to turn back
and then the next
note sounds

accelerates
to the brief coda
and cadence.

6

After a week of warm weather, I had gotten used to dry roads and
sidewalks. But a night's snow brought winter back briefly. Not the
light, downy snow of the city where my mother died, but the heavier
sort that falls when the temperature is in the 30s, near rain. The rasp
of the plow grating over the road in front. Just after sunset, snow still
hanging in the black trees.

~

And then the snow would have gone away
just as it had come
quietly almost
invisibly

for the days then would have lengthened
and the sun been lifted up above
the horizon line
and the moles
returned
to the woods

leaving their delicate trails
on the ground.

~

I was told that I would dream of her: that she would come to me and tell me that she was okay. Then I did dream of her, obedient child that I am, and asked her how she was. She said, smiling, "I am doing very well, except—" and then I woke up and didn't hear the last part of the sentence. I decided to place a period there, before *except*.

~

See the horizon line there?
Curve or edge?
For her, edge.

~

Gradually, spring came.
Camelspines, the hills cleaned themselves,
the earth turned brown, then green, and the sky filled

the ground, sprouting up from underneath.

~

Apple trees bloomed—then, in the first wind, littered the ground
white with their petals. Work continued in the backyard hole. It
was now the size of a football field, 35 feet deep with a shaft going
down to 70 feet. The dirt was uniform, sandy colored, not a stone
anywhere. The rain had stopped early in May, before the trees were
fully budded, and the exposed earth dried out and blew away in fine
sifted layers. Blew east, into the house, blew along the edge of the
driveway, into the street, blew north through the evergreens, turning
them misty gray.

~

I have become
    aware
of my heart
beat
    and the blood, pausing
in backstroke.

Twilight, and the field expands;
it follows
    that we walk   in single file

probing the new, warmer air.

That's why I don't stop
walking.

The ground had finally thawed. I drove north, to the town where I was born, the town where my mother was born, and went to the cemetery early. I pruned the apple tree blooming by my father's grave. The wind blew hard, snapping the branches from my grasp and loosing blossoms. The coffin was already there, resting over the hole. I asked the grave digger how big the hole was: 93 by 40 inches by 4 feet deep. It was a neat grave, very well squared off, no loose dirt. He drove the Bobcat up onto the back of a trailer and parked it down the hill, out of sight. My family arrived, and the deacon told his story and prayed his prayer. The undertaker waited for us to leave, but we didn't go. He finally began unwinding the blue ribbons that held the casket up. It went down easily, with one red rose on top. The next day, there was a small brown patch next to the green of my father's grave.

~

And what is the purpose of the wind

if not to keep the trees

clean. I've bent down time

and time again

to examine what falls.

~

Borrowing from infinity, much the same
as borrowing from zero.

In another room she
worked out her destiny

as here I grapple with the difference.
Stars she saw in her youth were already gone.

~

The next spring, I brought saplings to the gap in my small woods.
It will take twenty years to replace the nearly mature trees that were
taken. Twenty years to erase the view that this hole created at the
property line. Will the new soil hold its place? Perhaps it will erode
and form pockets and dips and small blank places that I will need to
come back and fill in later.

~

Field of kin
whit of kin

because of the whole of it
because of the songs

and the words
when they fail

Acknowledgments

I want to thank the writers who helped me get here: Becca Barniskis, Sharon Chmielarz, Janet Holmes, Amy McNamara, Anna Meek, John Minczeski, Veronica Patterson, K. Alma Peterson, Mary Jo Thompson, Christin Lore Weber, Susan Steger Welsh, Patricia Zontelli. Thanks also to Patricia Fargnoli for selecting my manuscript, to Jim Schley for his fine eye, and to Tupelo Press.

Other books from Tupelo Press

See our complete backlist at www.tupelopress.org